A
BEGINNER'S
GUIDE TO
CHRISTIANITY

For Those Seeking A Better Life

Chris Newell

xulon PRESS

A Beginner's Guide to Christianity
by Chris Newell

Printed in the United States of America

Library of Congress Control Number: 2002111276
ISBN 1-591601-87-8

Xulon Press
11350 Random Hills Road
Suite 800
Fairfax, VA 22030
(703) 279-6511
XulonPress.com

To order additional copies,
call 1-866-909-BOOK (2665).

Acknowledgements

I wish to extend my deepest appreciation to Dr. Merle Allison Johnson and Reverend Michael Mattox for their gracious and valuable expert advice. Their input, encouragement and support for this endeavor means more to me than they will ever know. Thanks, guys!

Foreword

❦

*H*aving written seven books for Revell, Tidings and Abingdon, I can feel some qualification for this introduction to Chris Newell's book. Another reason is that he was a parishioner for eleven years. After four years in retirement, I still vividly remember his and Paula's faithfulness, their troubles, and especially their blessings in two beautiful daughters.

In reading the manuscript, I continued to be amazed at Chris' ability to keep with his purpose. It is a remarkably quick and uncomplicated guideline to an overall look at our Christian faith. The key is that it was written by a young layman.

As a pastor, I looked for this book! I just didn't find

it in forty-seven years. Each similar attempt at a simple guide for seeking hearts became sidetracked and too complex. This is a valuable aid for those seeking to know why Chris and so many million more people call themselves, "Christian."

Dr. Merle Allison Johnson
Little Rock, Arkansas
2002

Contents

Chapter One

A Reason to Write

I am not a minister or a theologian and I'm certainly not making a claim to superior righteousness. I'm just a guy, who, for some reason, had a strong need to write this book. Let me start by telling you just a few things about this work and a bit about me.

This book is geared to a "target audience", for lack of a better term. If you are a strong Christian with a deep spiritual maturity then you are not the target audience, but I certainly welcome you to read further. However, I seem to run into a lot of people who can identify with the following:

"I know there is a God. I can believe that there is some kind of Supreme Being that is our Creator. However, I really have trouble with the concept of Jesus. I have a difficult time accepting the stories I hear from the New Testament such as the virgin birth, the miracles performed by Jesus and the resurrection. I also have a hard time accepting that Christianity is the only way to 'salvation'. There are many other religions in the world that all teach the great human virtues of love, peace and doing the right thing. I've attempted to read the Bible in the past and really didn't get very far nor did I get much out of it. I feel that I am a spiritual person and don't believe you have to be schooled in the Bible to be spiritual. I believe that if we are judged, then we are judged by what is in our heart and how we live our lives. I feel that I'm basically a good person with a good heart and I do my best to love others and do the right thing. I'm somewhat interested to know what attracts so many millions throughout the world to Christianity but honestly many Christians turn me off, particularly when they start preaching to me about what I should believe. Also, while I don't have any problem with people going to church, I've never seen the need for me to really get involved with a

particular church. I'm turned off and confused sometimes over so many Christian denominations if there
was only one Christ. I've also met many so-called
Christians who are hypocrites and I'm turned off by
televangelists milking people for money and people
who tell me I'm going to go to hell for not believing
what they believe."

Now, if you can relate to many of these statements,
then you are the target audience for this book. Please
understand that I'm not going to say you are wrong
and I'm not going to fill this book with the reasons
why you should believe the way I do. My point is to
address some of these questions and difficulties and
perhaps get you to think about some things in a different way. I will do this by outlining the basic concepts of Christianity. This may ultimately help you
work through your struggles on what to believe and
who to believe.

All I ask is that you read this book with an open
mind and forget about all of those I have eluded to
who may have turned you sour towards Christianity
in the past. I just want to help give you some things
to think about and I certainly won't try to cram anything down your throat.

This book is about the Christian faith but before we

get into the discussions about Christ, let's first talk about the basics of belief in God. All of the studies that have ever been done on faith have always determined that the vast majority of people in the world believe that there is a God. Actually, the percentage of atheists and agnostics in the world is very small. That is a very interesting place to start...why do so many people deep down believe in a supreme Creator? To me it is very difficult, and even intellectually lazy, to accept that we are here by accident. It is hard for most people to believe that all you see, feel, and experience in this world is strictly the result of random scientific happenings coming together at the right place at the right time.

Frankly, I know that there is just too much here to even conceive that there is no God. When I look at the stars at night, when I look at my children and feel the unexplainable love I have for them and they have for me, and when I see the beauty of nature and all of its intricacies—there is just no way that all of this is an accident!

Now, assuming that you're with me on this God concept, the next question that jumps off of the page to me is "If there is a God who created us, why did He create us?" Have you ever really given that question serious thought? If there is a God, why did He make us? Why are we here?

I've really given this question some serious pondering and the only answer I can come up with is that He created us for the purpose of loving communication. In other words, we have a Creator who seeks a relationship with us. When I was a kid and read the creation story in Genesis where it referred to God making us in His image, I thought that meant that God had a physical body that resembles ours. Now I've come to learn that "in God's image" means that we are beings of awareness and communication and have the ability to love and the need for relationships, just like God.

God made us out of love. If you believe that there is a God that created this universe as we know it, then please know that He is all-powerful, all-knowing, and, yes, He is also all-loving. You may question how an all-loving God can allow such suffering to exist on His earth, and we'll address this later in the book.

For now, I'm assuming that most of you are in agreement that there is a God who created the universe and is all-powerful. As we explore God further, we'll uncover some characteristics of God that are as real as any physical law in the universe that we have been able to scientifically prove.

Now I begin to set the stage to eventually discuss some important topics such as the purpose of Christ, what grace is and God's true purpose for our existence on this planet.

Let's start with Adam and Eve. You may be familiar with this story. Some people believe that Adam and Eve in the Garden of Eden literally happened the exact way it is portrayed in the Bible. Others believe that the Adam and Eve story wasn't written to be interpreted literally and instead regard the story as a beautiful parable to illustrate that when given the choice of God's will or our will, we will always choose our will.

Whether you believe the story literally or not is not important at this time, but the concepts that the story illustrates are very important. First of all, the story shows that God gave us free will. With free will, comes a price. But most importantly, the story introduces the concept of the "Original Sin".

If you understand "Original Sin," (note Sin with a capital "S", rather than the "sins" we commit, which is a small "s") then you will later understand the significance of Christ. Hang with me here, because these are ideas you may not have been exposed to before.

God is the creator of everything in the universe and is all-powerful. However, there is one thing that God cannot do. God cannot re-create Himself. Only God is holy and perfect and, although He created us in His image, He cannot re-create that which is perfect and holy. You see, anything less than God cannot be perfect or holy. It is physically and spiritually impossible!

The original Sin means that we are born into "Sin"— note with a capital "S"—which means that we are born into an existence of being separated from God. We are separated from God because only God is holy and we are not. Also, we are not born into this world with the desire to only do God's will for our lives. Given the choice, we will always ultimately slip into doing our will over God's, if they conflict.

I believe that God's original plan for our world was the Garden of Eden but He realized that we would always fail at completely obeying His will for our lives so the next best gift He could give us was free will. It is this freedom, this gift from God, that results in all of the good and all of the evil we do in this world.

One premise that we'll discuss later is that part of our freedom is the freedom to either love or reject God. When we later discuss the popular topic of heaven and hell, you'll see that God never rejects us. We reject Him.

So, what is God to do? He wants us in His loving presence for all eternity, but only that which is holy and righteous qualities for this. God loves us, but God also cannot stand to be close to sin. We are by nature born into separation from God but there must be a way to unite us with God. This is the purpose of Jesus Christ – to unite us with God. We are given the gift of God's eternal and loving presence even though we are not deserving of this gift.

This book will attempt to show you the basic principles of Jesus Christ and why Christ is necessary in the grand scheme of things. Many people declare, "I want to grow closer to God, but why do I have to go through Jesus first"? As you move through these pages with an open mind, I'll do my best to answer this question for you.

Please understand something. It is perfectly natural and OK to have doubts. Mother Teresa, the Apostle Paul, and John Wesley (the founder of the Methodist Church) all had doubts. You can still have faith and have doubts. In fact, as you develop your faith, it is not only your right but your duty to question and seek out answers.

Also understand this. God will never provide us with all of the answers while we're on this earth. Through prayer, study and personal experience your faith will grow, but to a certain extent you'll always have some doubts. God has set it up where our faith has to take over at some point. However, God did promise us in the Bible that if we seek Him out, we will find Him. If we look for Him, He will reveal Himself to us.

I have gone from a person who believed exactly who I described as my "target audience" for this book to someone who absolutely without a doubt believes in the teachings of Christianity. I have personally experienced a peace of mind that cannot be explained in words which is a result of growing closer to God through my faith.

I cannot offer you any advanced credentials such as a doctorate in theology. However, I can share with you what I've learned and experienced and maybe you can use this book as a catalyst to seek out those who are much more qualified than I to help you down your faith journey.

So where do I get my authority for the content of this book? Let's first start with the Holy Bible. If you have never read or studied the Bible or have only done so on a limited basis, you may find the next chapter helpful. The purpose of this book is not to provide you with a detailed accounting of the history of Christianity, but rather to summarize and introduce some key concepts that may guide you down your spiritual walk.

You are a spiritual person and perhaps you have the desire to learn more. This desire is a gift from God. As you read through these pages, remember that you have a Creator who loves you and wants to grow closer to you. You'll see how Christ fits into God's plan.

He was from a very poor family and although we know he was schooled on the scriptures, he probably didn't have much formal education. As an adult, he was a carpenter with little money and was probably without home ownership. His literary skills are not defined. With the exception of the days following his birth, he never traveled more than 200 miles from his birthplace in his entire life, which was only about 33 years. And by the way, he lived 2000 years ago. Yet, there is no arguing that Jesus has been the most influential person ever to walk the face of the earth. If you disagree, check today's date. Our very calendar is based on his life and death.

This alone should pique your interest as to "why Jesus"? Who was this man and what happened 2000 years ago to result in a religion with roughly 20% of the today's entire world population as followers?

Chapter Two

A Quick Journey Through the Book of All Books

❦

*T*he Bible is the most read and the most translated book in the history of the world. This alone may fascinate you, if for no other reason than from just a literary study point of view. The Bible is full of stories and every human experience you can possibly imagine. There is almost no element of our human condition that is not addressed somewhere in the Bible.

Although the Bible is a series of many different stories, writings, praises, and poems coming from vastly different people over hundreds of years, there is an overall theme and a beginning and an end. The beginning of the Bible is Genesis with the creation of the world and the ending is Revelation with the ending of this world. The overall theme throughout the entire Bible is God's relationship with humankind.

The Old Testament is a collection of writings, which tell about God's relationship to the ancient Hebrew people. Most scholars agree that Moses wrote the first book of the Bible called "Genesis", which is also the first of the first five books in the Old Testament known as the Pentateuch (meaning "five volumed book").

Genesis begins with "In the beginning God created the heavens and the earth" and quickly moves into the story of Adam and Eve and their offspring. There is the story of Noah and his Ark and then the plot moves quickly to Abraham and Sarah. To make a long story short, God chooses Abraham to be the father of the Hebrew nation. Even though he and Sarah are old (way beyond her child-bearing years), God enables her to become pregnant with Isaac, whose offspring are the beginning of the tribes of Israel. These people were later called "Hebrews."

The Hebrews were few in number and circumstances led them to move to Egypt, where they became slaves to the Pharaoh. God chose the Hebrew Moses to lead his people out of Egyptian bondage. I suggest you read Exodus, the second book of the Old Testament, for a detailed account of the story of Moses and how he led the Hebrew people away with God's direction.

For an estimated 40 years, the Hebrews wandered the desert in search of their "promised land". During this time God revealed the Ten Commandments, as well as the other detailed commandments of Jewish law to Moses. These instructions or laws were given to help the Hebrews worship and live as God's holy people. He had chosen them for a special purpose. The next three books of the Old Testament (Leviticus, Numbers and Deuteronomy) outline the detailed instructions from God and tell about His initial relationship with these Hebrew people as they move toward the land of Canaan. There they eventually establish the kingdom of Israel. They are called Israelites after this period, named after their father Jacob, also known as Israel.

Let me pause here to tell you why a study of the history of Israel is so important. God revealed Himself to the Hebrews and Jesus is a descendent of Abraham.

You have to study both the Old and New Testament to realize that God had a plan from the beginning for the coming of Jesus the Christ into the world. This really started with Abraham and his children.

After Deuteronomy, the Old Testament moves into a series of historical books. These books tell stories about the kings of Israel and God's interaction with the nation of Israel. Some kings were good, and some kings were not so good. As you read this section of the Old Testament, you realize that time and time again Israel goes against the instructions of God and He still forgives them and takes care of them. As Israel became a larger kingdom, they had to wage war almost constantly against enemies from all around.

One of the great kings during the history of Israel was King David. This is the same David who, as a young boy, slew the very large enemy warrior named Goliath (you may have heard this story). After this, David became a great warrior and eventually king. Israel flourished under David's reign and David's son, Solomon, was the successor king who took Israel to a level it had never been before.

Solomon built the first great temple for worship and economically things were booming. But Solomon ended up somewhat losing touch with the true will of God and his legacy left a nation that soon fell to enemies and ultimately the Israelites were taken over and scattered in exile throughout the lands. Many years later, they were allowed to come back to their homeland and eventually rebuild their temple. Eventually they became subjects of the Roman Empire, which was the situation during the time of Christ.

After the historical books, there is a book called "Job" which is a story of one man's suffering and his one on one confrontation with God. This is an amazing story, which addresses many key issues.

Then we move into the Psalms and Proverbs, which are songs and poems primarily used to praise and worship God in their services. Many of these writings are absolutely beautiful and most of them are written by King David and King Solomon. These types of writings continue with the next two books called Ecclesiastes and Song of Songs.

Then we get into the remaining books of the Old Testament, which are primarily a collection of writings from "prophets" who were considered special spokespeople for God. The true prophets were given Divine insight and wrote about what God had told them and what they believed would happen in the future. Some of the most revealing characteristics of God come from Isaiah and Jeremiah, for example.

The New Testament is all about Jesus Christ. If you have never read the Bible my recommendation is to start with the New Testament. Reading the Bible can be very difficult at first, but as you grow spiritually you grow in your understanding of the scriptures.

There is a never-ending debate in the Christian community about how literally one should interpret the writings of the Bible. Some believe that every word of the Bible should be taken literally at face value and others believe that it is more important to glean the truth from the Bible rather than all of the intricate facts. The discussions of this debate are beyond the scope of this book, but let me say that when you read the Bible it is very important to understand who wrote the scripture, when it was written and the culture at the time, and to whom they were writing. Remember that none of the writers of the scriptures had any idea that their writings would end up in the compilation known as the Holy Bible. Be very careful taking scripture out of context and be watchful of those who do.

The first four books of the New Testament—Matthew,

Mark, Luke and John—tell basically the same story four different times. All of these books are about the life and teachings of Jesus and these books are known as the "Gospels". Matthew and John were part of the original twelve disciples of Jesus and lived and traveled with Him for three years. Therefore, their writings are first-hand eyewitness accounts of what happened.

Be patient when you read these four books straight through for the first time because it is somewhat repetitive. That's OK, because as you are reading the Bible you are being filled with God's Spirit (more on this later) and your understanding of Christ is growing.

The fifth book in the New Testament is called "Acts". This book tells the story of the beginnings of the Christian movement, starting with the disciples after the crucifixion, resurrection and ascension of Jesus into heaven. Then we meet a character named Saul.

Unlike the disciples who were, for the most part, basically uneducated hard-working blue-collar guys, Saul was a well-educated person dedicated to destroying the Christian movement. The early Christians were subject to much persecution just for their beliefs. Saul was present at the stoning of a Christian martyr named Stephen and was secretly very impressed with the courage, character and faith shown by Stephen as he faced his death.

That wasn't enough to sway Saul, however, so one day on the road to Damascus Saul was blinded by a great light and heard the voice of Christ asking why Saul was persecuting His people. Saul's encounter with Jesus Christ caused him to completely turn around and when he regained his sight he began using his Greek name, Paul, and dedicated the rest of his life to being a "slave to Christ", as he put it.

Paul was a missionary with a zeal no one had ever seen before. He started many Christian churches and kept in touch with them by writing letters. The next several books in the Bible that follow Acts are letters written by Paul to the various Christian churches throughout the Roman world. His letters address many of the Christian concepts that we'll talk about later in this book such as salvation, grace, sin, faith and love.

The first letter from Paul after Acts in the New Testament is Romans. This book is an excellent overview of the basic Gospel, which is God's plan for salvation and righteousness for all people, Jew and Gentile (non-Jew) alike. We will be referring to Paul's writings quite a bit in this book as we address some key areas of the Christian faith. Paul definitely helps clarify the purpose of Christ and is the most predominant writer of the New Testament.

After Paul's letters, there is a book called "James", written by the brother of Jesus. At first James did not believe in Jesus and even challenged His mission but later became one of the most prominent leaders in the church. Then there are the two books written by the disciple Peter, who I must confess is my favorite disciple. When you read about Peter in the Gospels, you can't help but like his "shoot from the hip" method of operation. His style was, "ready, fire, aim"!

The next three small books are written by the apostle John followed by Jude and then finally Revelation. We'll discuss Revelation a bit later, but suffice it to say at this time that Revelation is the most misunderstood, misquoted and misinterpreted book in the Bible and it is very difficult to read and understand. It's basic message is that Christians will go through times of trial and tribulation with good versus evil and, in the end, God wins.

After you read this book, you should immediately

begin your journey by reading and studying the New Testament. Eventually, you'll need support. It's a very good idea to get into a Bible study group with like-minded people and to read books that help explain the stories and teachings of the Bible.

Yes, the Bible was written, assembled, translated and interpreted by humans but you'll see as you continue to read this book why we Christians sincerely believe that the Bible is the Holy Word of God. I personally don't believe that God dictated to the writers of the Bible word for word, but the Bible is definitely inspired and supported by God. God is much bigger than the Bible itself but be assured that God intended this book to be His primary written communication to us. All of the other Christian literature in the world should merely expand upon the concepts and teachings in the Holy Scriptures.

As you read the Bible, let me caution you that some of the scriptures are disturbing, particularly in the Old Testament. In the Old Testament, God is sometimes portrayed as angry, vengeful and He often punishes His people. This is when you seek out Biblical scholars to explain these troubling passages. I find only a very few scriptures to be disturbing but I'm no longer disturbed when I remember that this is the same God who loved the world so much that He sent

His only son into the world to die for our sins. You've heard that sentence blurted out by Christians in the past, and by the end of this book you'll understand what it really means.

Another problem you may face is that sometimes you'll have difficulty understanding the meaning behind what you are reading. The Bible is that way sometimes. As you grow closer to God, you grow in your understanding and the scriptures become clearer to you. I remember on several occasions reading something later in my spiritual walk that made complete sense to me when it made no sense during a previous reading. As you'll also see in the upcoming pages, this increased understanding is part of being filled with God's Holy Spirit.

I encourage you to seek out God by reading and studying the Bible. Remember, He will reveal Himself to you and your faith will grow over time through prayer, study, worship, service and interaction with other Christians.

Chapter Three

From the Written Word to the Living Word

❧

So who was/is Jesus? What is the "Trinity"? What is the Holy Spirit? I will attempt to answer those questions right now. But before I begin, let me say that you'll have to read the Gospels (the first four books of the New Testament), the Acts and some of Paul's letters (especially Romans) to begin to really understand Jesus Christ.

Jesus the man on this earth was a part of God in human form. He was and is the Son of God, meaning that He was born into this world as a human being fully capable of experiencing everything about the human existence. As a human, He is the Son of God and He constantly refers to God as His Father in heaven. However, Jesus was and is Divine as well, meaning He is actually a part of God incarnate (in human form).

It is difficult to understand how the Son of God can also be God in human form. Now that you are questioning how I can believe this about just another human being who walked the face of the earth, I might as well go ahead and really stretch your mind and talk about the Trinity.

The Trinity is a difficult concept to wrap your brain around at first. Christians believe that all of the evidence from the Scriptures and the personal experiences with God point to our one God being made up of three distinct parts or "Persons". There is God the Father (our Creator in heaven), God the Son (Jesus Christ) and God the Holy Spirit (God's Spirit working and manifesting inside of us and flowing through His creation to guide its development). This is what we refer to as the "Trinity".

Christians definitely believe in one God. Although our complex God is made up of three Persons, they are simultaneously One Being. Think of a three-leaf clover...each leaf is different, but all part of one clover.

A "triune" God makes for a much more personal and loving God. The Trinity shows us God as three loving Persons, each totally giving and loving to the other part. When Jesus came to earth, God revealed the Second Person of Himself to us in human form. After the human Jesus ascended into heaven,the Holy Spirit (or God's Third Person) was revealed to us.

You see, the coming of Christ was part of a deep self-revelation from God. Through Christ, God began showing us His true makeup, which is love. The result of this harmonious love in God's three Persons is our creation because God has the desire to share this great love. We'll talk more about the Trinity and the Holy Spirit in a later chapter.

God knew that in order to relate to humans He would need to send the Second Person of the Trinity in human form. One time I was very distressed and my faith was being tested. I was looking at all of the suffering in the world and questioning why things were the way they were. Why did God set things up like this? In my venting, I said to my wife that most of the time I just can't "relate" to God. I then told her that I could easily relate to Christ. I found it very hard to get mad at a guy who just came to earth to suffer right along with us and who ended up dying on a cross. My wife, Paula, then said something very profound. She said, "Chris, that's the way it's supposed to be. You're supposed to be able to relate to Christ better than God. God is God and Christ was God as a human being. That is why He was sent, so we could relate to God in human terms."

If you want to know what God is really like and what He really thinks about things, read the teachings of Jesus in the Gospels. Jesus said repeatedly that He was speaking on behalf of His Father.

Let's go back and talk about Jesus the man for a moment. Prior to His birth the Israelites were expecting a messiah, or savior to be born. The prophets repeatedly wrote about a messiah in the Old Testament and the Jews were waiting for someone to come along and lead them out from under the Roman oppression. They were looking for and expecting a political messiah, a great king like David.

Little did they know that the messiah and savior of

not just the Jews but of the world would be born to a very poor couple. What's more, instead of coming to earth as a rich and powerful king, He came as a humble servant. He came to serve, not be served. He associated with the lowest of the low—with the poor, the sick and the despised, as well as a few who had money and power but were spiritually needy.

He came to this earth for one purpose—to do the will of God. He was the only human to ever do this and the only human to be without sin. He knew that His purpose was to recruit a handful of disciples to travel with Him to teach about God and He also knew that His ultimate purpose was to die on the cross and be resurrected to triumph over death and therefore to triumph over our sins. You see, He had to be human to suffer and die but He had to be God to be without sin and to triumph over death in resurrection. Only a "God/man" could accomplish this. Any other human born into "Sin" would be incapable of bearing our sins and making us right with God by dying for us.

So why should we believe all that Jesus said about Himself? First, consider the miracles. Jesus healed the sick time and again. Word spread of this and there was no denying that hundreds of people followed Him around because of His healing power. There were numerous witnesses to these miracles and even the enemies of Jesus (the elite of the Jewish church who felt threatened) couldn't deny what they had witnessed.

Witnesses also saw Him bring Lazarus back from the dead, turn water into wine and walk on water. The sheer number of eyewitnesses to His miracles demonstrate the credibility of these stories in the Bible.

Next, if you believe in Christianity, you'll have to believe in the teachings of Jesus. I truly believe that if God were to speak to us directly, He would say the same things that Christ preached. These teachings can be disturbing because quite often it is much harder to abide by the teachings of Christ than other religions of the world.

For example, Jesus says to turn the other cheek. If someone wants to spit on you, let him spit on you again. Love your enemy. Forgive others. Don't judge others without first judging yourself. When you are fasting for God, don't let anyone know. When you are tithing and donating money, don't let anyone know. Jesus said, "Don't let the left hand know what the right hand is doing."

Be humble. Give to others and expect nothing in

return. Be a servant to all humankind. Love God with all of your heart and all of your soul. Even if you didn't act upon your lustful desire, you have still sinned if you have lusted in your heart. Seek first the kingdom of God, rather than money or material possessions.

When you read Jesus' sermon on the mount in the book of Matthew, it really hits you between the eyes. Jesus does not mince words. Many things in the Bible are subject to interpretation but the teachings of Jesus are cut and dried. Christians are also called to be set apart. We are to love our enemies when others can't understand this. We are to give to that street corner bum when others think we're crazy. We are to forgive those who hurt us, when others are out for vengeance. We are to practice humility, which is the hardest thing of all. We are to follow the example of Christ and try to be as Christ was. That's what it means to be a Christian.

For almost everybody, this requires change. However, there's a difference once you commit to Christ and Paul writes a lot about this. If it were all about just being a good person and following God's rules, we would lose every time. We are all sinners and our sinful nature would eventually win the inner conflict that would be within us. However, when we turn our lives over to Christ, something happens within us and we actually become filled with God's Holy Spirit as the Bible says. This Spirit manifests a change within us whereby we are no longer fighting against doing the right thing and fighting against abiding by the teachings of Jesus. We actually want to live like Christ. While trying to live a life according to the example of Christ is difficult, the by-product is an inner peace and joy that comes straight from God.

Do Christians still sin and have hardships? Of course! Christians continue to be people who will still succumb to all of the frailties of our human condition. But, your heart is changed forever and you are a different person. You will begin to live the life God has planned for you. There is no greater joy than enthusiastically living your life for Christ.

I mentioned that Christians are still people, with all the imperfections that come with being a human being. I've heard some people say that they like what they read and hear about Christ, it's just that they don't like Christians. Truthfully, I can relate to this because unfortunately quite often the fanatical minority are the most outspoken. This is true of most religions in the world. The fanatical so-called Christians are no different than the fanatical Islamic fundamentalists in many ways. There are also people who profess to be Christians who openly judge others and are even caught doing unethical and criminal things in the name of God. This can certainly cause the non-Christian to have a negative view of "Christians" if this is all they see.

Let me make two important points in addressing this. First, never confuse Christians with Christ. All Christians are imperfect and fallible because all people are. All churches have inner politics and bickering and could occasionally be subject to scandal because that goes along with being made up of people. But never confuse a televangelist getting caught stealing money or a fanatic insisting that you're going to hell with the truth of God and Christ!

Second, focus on the vast majority of Christians in the world who do good things. Look at the missionaries and the hospitals and the Christian charities. Look at the mission work done by nearly every church on a local, national and global level. These people, despite their human shortcomings, are doing Christ's work. Their work is quietly supported by the tithes and offerings of average, normal, church-going people.

Let's get back to why you would consider the belief of Jesus Christ as the Son of God.

We've talked about the numerous eyewitnesses to the miracles. How can a 21st century rational person actually believe that Jesus performed these miracles? First, you have to logically believe that if there is a God who is the author of this entire physical universe including all of the physical laws that make up the universe, surely this God would have the power to alter these physical laws in order to serve His need. Wouldn't you think? I mean, if you can believe that God created all matter as we know it, and all of the scientific laws that we have been able to prove so far, it's inconceivable to me that you would also believe that this same God would be incapable of altering these laws and performing "miracles"!

But, from a worldly perspective, consider this. During the time of Jesus, something had to happen time and again for that many credible eyewitnesses to concur that Jesus had supernatural abilities. Moreover, there were so many threatened by Him that if there were any way to prove him a fraud His enemies certainly would have found a way.

The same holds true for the resurrection. For some reason, there are those who can easily believe that

Christ performed miracles but that He could not have risen from the dead. Before we discuss the resurrection of Christ, let me make two rather strong statements. First, you must acknowledge that if something is the truth then it is not a lie. If something is not the truth, then it is a lie. There really isn't any gray area here. So, in your search for the truth, you will either end up believing that the accountings of Jesus' life as portrayed in the Gospels are either the truth or they are a lie. The entire writings of the New Testament are either the truth or the biggest lie ever to be told to mankind.

We will discuss the significance of the resurrection in the chapter on grace but for now let's briefly discuss the account in the Bible leading up to it. When the Romans came and arrested Jesus, the disciples scattered. They were terrified. There were many Roman soldiers and Jewish elders who took Jesus to a mockery of a trial in the middle of the night and the disciples were scared that their lives were threatened by their association with Jesus.

The Jewish Chief Priests wanted Jesus dead, primarily because He was gaining so many followers that it was causing a huge stir among the people of Jerusalem. They felt that He was definitely not their messiah and that their ability to peacefully exist and practice their religion under Roman authority was in jeopardy. The Romans at the time let the Jews practice their religion as long as they paid their hefty taxes to Caesar and didn't get out of line.

It was decided that Jesus would be crucified for treason against Caesar. Every Roman and Jewish law in the book was thrown out in His case. Under normal circumstances, there would have been no way that Jesus would have received the death penalty so quickly and without any proof of their charge.

When you read the New Testament there are numerous references to Old Testament scripture, which gave prophecies about Jesus that came true. In fact, it is absolutely amazing when you do a cross-reference. One of the prophecies about the death of the messiah in the Old Testament is that no bones would be broken. During crucifixions, it was very common for the guards to break the legs of the one being crucified to expedite their death. The New Testament says that the guards did this to the other two criminals that were crucified along with Jesus, but when they came to Jesus they noted that He was already dead. Instead, one of the guards pierced His side with a spear to confirm that He was actually dead. The Old Testament scripture also said, "They will look on the one they have pierced".

There were two men named Joseph of Arimathea and Nicodemus who were well-to-do Jewish leaders that secretly followed and believed in Jesus. They obtained permission from the Romans to take His body down from the cross and wrap it with spices and many strips of linen to anoint the body for burial, which was the Jewish custom at the time.

His body was placed in a tomb and a very large boulder was rolled over the entrance. Guards were placed outside. This all happened on a Friday. The next day was their Sabbath (Saturday) so no one tried to visit the tomb. But early Sunday morning while it was still dark, a long-time follower of Jesus named Mary Magdalene went to the tomb and saw that the boulder had been removed from the entrance. She ran back to Peter and John crying that someone had taken the Lord's body.

When Peter and John ran to the tomb to see for themselves, they found the strips of linen in the tomb but no body. The disciples went back to their homes and Mary remained outside the tomb crying. The scriptures say that as she wept, she looked into the tomb and saw two angels in white, seated where Jesus' body had been, one at the head and one at the foot. They asked Mary why she was crying and she told them that they had taken her Lord and she didn't know where they had put Him.

At that moment, Jesus appeared behind her and called her by name. He told her to go tell the disciples that He was returning to His Father in heaven. When she ran back to tell the disciples, they of course did not believe her. However, later that evening as they were gathered in their upper room to pray, Jesus appeared before them.

Read the Gospels and you'll see that Jesus later appeared to His disciples and to many others before ascending into heaven. The disciples didn't believe that Jesus had risen from the dead until they saw Him personally. The Bible also mentions that Jesus made appearances to many others before His ascension.

The disciples then knew that Jesus had triumphed over death and that only the Son of God, as He claimed to be, could have done this. However, as you'll see when you read the book of Acts, it wasn't until a later time at Pentecost that the disciples truly understood the purpose of Jesus' life, death and resurrection and what it meant for them and the world.

The disciples then realized that He was truly both human and God. God sent the human part to suffer and relate to human beings because He was sent to save human beings. However, only the Divine can be without Sin and bear the burdens of our sins.

I can only pray that this brief introduction into the life of Christ will at least motivate you to read the New Testament and try to get a better understanding of how Jesus fits into God's total picture as He relates to us. I hope that the next few chapters will be interesting to you and perhaps help you come to a better understanding of the basics of the Christian faith.

Chapter Four

Faith and Hope

What is faith? Faith is the bridge between what we know exists and what we know must exist. Let's say you get on an airplane. Would you dare consider flying with a pilot who didn't have a pilot's license? I would think not. Now, the last time you flew in an airplane did you ask the pilot to show you his license? I bet you didn't. You were using your faith. You knew that because he was flying for a commercial airline that he just had to have a license. You knew that this license must exist, even though you didn't see it.

When you look at the physical part of the world we are able to experience with our senses, you know that this universe exists. When you consider that this universe had to have been created by a higher power than us, then you know that God must exist. It is faith that has taken you from point A to point B. From believing in something you can see, hear, taste, touch or smell to something you know must exist based on the evidence.

Why do you suppose that God set up this whole plan based on faith? Why doesn't He just open up the skies and reveal Himself to us? Have you ever thought, "Just give me a sign, God"? And why does the Bible say there are such consequences for not having faith? And why should you have faith in a God that you can't see? And why doesn't God speak directly to us from the burning bush, like He did for Moses? And why doesn't God simply explain to us all of the questions we have for Him, such as why we're here and why there is so much unexplained suffering in this world?

Faith is believing in something. Most people have faith in something or someone. The definition of total despair is not having faith or hope in anything. We're going to talk about the Christian faith and we're also going to talk about hope. Most people who commit suicide have given up on ever having any hope. There are so many people who have lost faith and hope. This condition is one of the saddest in the world. It doesn't have to be that way for them.

Let's start with the question of why God based His relationship with us on faith. Because it is based on faith, we'll never have all of the answers while we're on this earth. I can only share with you what I think, based on my personal experience.

First, there are some misconceptions about faith. There are many who believe that when bad things happen to them, it is a result of a lack of faith. "If I had prayed harder and believed more, my loved one would have been healed." Faith is not correlated with direct results from God in that fashion. We'll talk more about faith healing in the chapter on prayer but suffice it to say at this time that God doesn't directly cause bad things to happen to you or intentionally not heal you because of a lack of faith.

It is also important not to confuse faith with feelings. Feelings come and go. Faith has nothing to do with experiencing a temporary religious high. Faith is a core belief that has to be nurtured and strengthened over time. Faith is not knowledge. God has intentionally not revealed everything to us because

He is more interested in our faith in Him rather than knowledge of Him. God based His relationship with us on our faith in Him. He couldn't give us all of the answers where we would understand Him if He wanted to. God is so vast and so beyond our comprehension that our relationship with Him has to be based on faith.

Furthermore, having faith is good for us because it is tied to humility. We have to humble ourselves to have faith in something we can't see or completely understand. Christ said that we should be "childlike" in our faith. Even if you are the most brilliant physicist in the world with an understanding of the physical laws of our universe that few will ever have, God wants your faith to be that of a child's.

Another reason that God based His relationship with us on faith is that faith is one of the strongest forces known. There is no force more powerful than one's strong faith in something. When you experience a growth in your faith, you'll see what it is like to grow closer to God. It is part of the natural order of things as your faith grows. As you grow closer to God, your faith grows because of this and you begin a cycle that moves you closer and closer to God while your faith grows stronger and stronger. But all the time realize that faith is our choice. God has given us free will to either believe or not.

Now I would like to talk for a moment about the importance of the church in strengthening and maintaining your faith. Many people don't see the need for corporate worship and feel that they can grow spiritually within themselves. I used to think this way until I became actively involved in a church and realized what church is all about.

First of all, although any organization made up of people is never going to be perfect, the church is our only way of nurturing our faith with others and passing our faith to our children. Even if your faith is strong, it is like a coal in a charcoal grill. If your single burning coal falls out, it will eventually go out. It has to be burning with other coals in order to stay burning.

The church is so important for many reasons. First, it is your means of worship. If you become a Christian, you will want to worship God. It's just that simple. The church is your means to worship God. There are so many Christian denominations because there are so many types of Christians who prefer different ways to worship and learn. This should not be a hindrance to your faith but rather a source to strengthen you. Since there are so many Christian denominations, find one that fits your personality and go with it!

Attending church also provides you with a disciplined regimen, which pleases God. Quite often we need to be forced to do something and make it a routine in order to make it an integral part of our lives. I am a member of the United Methodist Church and the founder of the Methodist Church, John Wesley, was very "methodical" in how he lived his spiritual life and hence the name, "Methodist".

The church is also how you learn. A good Sunday school class or Bible study will give you the forum to learn from others. I've never learned much from myself. It takes those around me to teach me something.

Perhaps the most underrated benefit you'll receive from a church environment is Christian fellowship. When you develop strong friendships within the church, there is a bond that is unlike any other kind of friendship. I can't begin to explain to you the value of the friendships my family has developed at our church over the years. And let me tell you from first hand experience that when your chips are down, the support you'll receive from your dedicated church friends will blow your mind.

All of these elements of a church go to strengthen your faith. When you actually experience faith in action, your faith gets stronger. A nurturing church environment should help you grow. That is a major goal of any Christian church. If you jump in and get involved, the rewards will come back to you ten times over. Just like your involvement in anything else, you'll get out of it what you put into it.

A church teaches you all of the fundamentals that will go toward your spiritual growth such as worship, prayer, service, and tithing. If you have a family, then I guarantee that the church will strengthen your family bond. Your marriage will be stronger. Your children will have a special bond with you, even stronger than before, if you get them involved in church activities.

We've talked a bit about what faith is and isn't and how faith can be strengthened. What are some detriments to faith? How can your faith be challenged and weakened? What keeps you from growing any further in your faith right now?

Earlier I mentioned that it is OK to have doubts. You can certainly have doubts and have faith. But we first need to take an honest look at ourselves to determine the source of some of our doubts. For example, I read once about a famous scientist who indicated that he honestly wished he could buy into the Christian faith but that his intellect just would not allow him to do it. When he was pressed a bit harder from one of his theologian friends, it was discovered that if he publicly accepted Christianity he would be a source of ridicule by his atheist scients colleagues. Deep down, he wasn't willing to accept the worldly consequences of declaring his Christian faith.

An acquaintance of mine had expressed that he just couldn't buy into the whole "Jesus thing". When pressed a little harder, it became clear that he didn't want to give up his hard-drinking, womanizing lifestyle. Quite often we know that a change of faith would result in a change in our lives and most of us are resistant to change. Procrastination, complacency and deep down fear of change are probably the greatest barriers to growing your faith.

Life also has a way of challenging your faith from time to time. I've certainly had my faith challenged to the point of questioning whether a loving God actually exists. When we're hurting and in despair, it is perfectly natural to blame God. We figure that He is all-powerful and therefore able to prevent this suffering we're experiencing. I've had screaming fits at

God before and, in retrospect, I think He understood.

I will tell you this, however. Even though you'll go through times where you just can't feel God's love, He is there and He is closer to you during your suffering than any other time in your life. And if you just turn over all of your pain to God, He will reveal Himself to you in a way that you have never before experienced. Remember that Christ is suffering right along with you. That is why He came to earth, suffered as a human and died.

I'm reminded of the story of a mother whose child was severely injured in an automobile wreck and put in a coma. The mother would go home just long enough to shower and change clothes but otherwise would spend every waking and occasional sleeping moment by the bed of her child. When others tried to encourage her to go home to get some rest, she merely said that she had to be near her child. Even though the child had no way of knowing she was there, she had to be there beside him during his time of suffering and need. God is the same way with us. Whether or not we realize it, He is closest to us during our time of despair. That is why those suffering throughout the world are the ones who are actually closest to God.

It took me a long time of reading and studying the Bible to finally figure out that the central theme is that God just wants us to completely put our lives into His hands. We don't have to bear our burdens by ourselves any more. Sometimes we have to hit rock bottom before we learn to "let go and let God" because we are all naturally control freaks. We actually believe that we are in charge of our own destiny! It is an incredible peace that overcomes you when you realize that you are not in control at all. You don't have to be in control! When you put your life in God's hands, this is the beginning of your faith journey.

God doesn't expect any kind of grandiose accomplishment out of your life. He expects you to love Him and to love others. Mother Teresa was once asked how she could continue her work in Calcutta, India with the sickest and poorest people in the world. No matter what good she did, there was always much more suffering than she could possibly alleviate. She replied by saying that she wasn't called to be successful. She was only called to be faithful.

I mentioned earlier that faith is an act of humility. It is an act of giving. We are "giving" God our faith in exchange for the grace and love He gives us. Too many people look at religion as "What's in it for me?" Or, "That belief really doesn't do anything for me." Christianity is a hard religion because it's a religion of humility. You are to humble yourself before God and to serve, not be served. Christians realize that this is supposed to be a life of giving rather than what you can take out of life. In other word's, it's not what you've got that's important; it's what you give. Frankly, that's a hard sale sometimes. But the benefit is a personal loving relationship with Jesus Christ that gives you a peace of mind unlike anything else.

Faith grows through prayer, worship, serving others, sharing your faith with others and hearing about their faith, and your own personal experience. When you experience God's spirit within you, you'll know that this is something that is very real. God has revealed Himself to me in this way and I've seen it time and time again in other people. This experience alone is enough to strengthen your faith and give you hope. And it's certainly good enough for me.

Chapter 5

Grace and Salvation

*D*o you know what grace is? You have heard this word many times in your life, but could you define it in terms of the Christian faith? Grace and salvation are perhaps the most important doctrines of the Christian faith. We have laid the foundation and now we're about to really get into what it's all about.

Grace is unmerited favor. It's an undeserved gift. Grace is the ultimate gift we receive from God by accepting what Jesus Christ did for us.

What is salvation? Many people equate salvation with going to heaven. There have been many Christians throughout the ages who have interpreted salvation as their admission ticket to heaven or as an insurance policy just in case a heaven exists. So often, the focus is on walking down the aisle to the altar and proclaiming that you believe in Jesus and then you are "saved" and that's all you have to do. There is no focus on what you do beyond this point. There are also a lot of Christians who focus on fearing God and spend their life trying to earn favor with God to assure their salvation.

Actually the last approach is truly misguided. Yes, salvation is being "saved" and being accepted into God's eternal kingdom but it's more than that. Salvation is being made whole with God right now, while you are on earth, and living your life in close communion with God.

So, how are we "saved"? We are saved by grace, not by our works. This is a very important statement so I'll say it again. We are saved by God's grace, not by our works! If we are saved by grace, how to we get grace? Why do we need grace?

Before we get into grace, let's talk about Sin and sins just for a moment. Recall from Chapter 1 that because only God is perfect and holy, we are born into an existence of being separated from God. We are separated from God because we are all sinners. Sin takes on many forms. It is selfishness, evil, doing our will over God's will and so forth. Paul declared that every single person is a sinner. We are all guilty as charged. Sin has the effect of jamming the frequencies between God and us. Our sins get in the way of our loving relationship with God.

Many people look at all of the evil in the world and the evil within themselves and blame Satan or "the devil". While I believe there is a devil, I don't blame Satan for all of the evil in the world. I actually blame humankind. We are naturally sinners and the chaos in this world is the result of a planet controlled by sinners. "The devil made me do it" mentality simply doesn't fly with me.

God actually knew from the beginning that we would be imperfect creatures. He loves us so much anyway, that He came up with a way to reconcile us with Him. He did it based on His nature and based on His fundamental principles of the universe He created. He couldn't have done it any other way.

Knowing that we are sinners, He gave us His gift of grace. Grace is our way to be restored with God and to be delivered from the bondage of sin and death that we have created for ourselves. The way He chose to give us this grace was by loving sacrifice. He sent his only Son into the world to die for us.

Think about that just for a minute. How could God send His Son into this world knowing that He would die a horrible death? How could a loving God be a part of that? The answer to that is that He loved us so much that He was willing to make that incredible sacrifice. Christ loved us so much and He loved His father in heaven so much that His only will was to do God's will, even if it meant dying a horrific death. Can you imagine loving humankind so much that you would allow them to kill your child if it meant that humanity would have the opportunity to be saved by accepting this great sacrifice?

I hope you are beginning to understand the significance of the sacrifice that God and Jesus Christ made for us. Christ had to die to be resurrected to show the world that by dying, He won. By losing, He ultimately triumphed over death so that we would ultimately triumph over death as well. So, we don't have to do anything to obtain salvation; it has already been done for us! All we have to do is acknowledge and accept this great sacrifice and we'll have God's gift of grace.

We have defined grace as unmerited favor; God's gift

to us that we didn't do anything to earn. Let's talk further about grace. I would like to discuss three types of grace: prevenient grace, justifying grace and sanctifying grace.

We have already said that the sacrifice has already been done and grace is already there for the taking. This is prevenient grace. Prevenient grace means that this grace existed before we were born. We are born into Sin and into a state of being separated from God but we are also born with the gift of prevenient grace.

Every person has a small voice inside of them calling them to God. This seed that God planted within you is part of His prevenient grace. You didn't do anything to get that little voice. You do have to respond to it, but this inner need inside of you to seek out God is part of God's prevenient grace. He knows that you need this grace, so He gives you the thirst that needs to be quenched. That faint little knock that you are hearing is God calling you into a relationship with Him through Jesus Christ.

We have said that grace is a gift for you from God, but remember God's other great gift to us is free will. He doesn't force His grace down our throats. We have to accept this grace. This is called justifying grace and it requires us to do something. Justifying grace means that in order to get God's grace, we have to accept this gift. This wonderful gift of eternal salvation is there for the taking, but we have to accept it.

When Paul wrote and taught about this, the primary criticism from the Jewish elders was that this was too easy. The idea of eternal salvation being ours just by accepting and believing in Christ as your savior just seems too easy. Actually it is very easy but it is amazing how many people reject this grace! We are forgiven for our sins but we must accept the grace given to us and realize that it is only by God's grace and Christ's sacrifice that we are good enough to deserve eternal salvation. Nothing that we could ever do on our own would be good enough to deserve eternal life in heaven.

We say that accepting this grace is easy but maybe it's not so easy. Once again, we are called to be humble. We are required to believe that grace is not something we earn or deserve. By humbling ourselves, we accept this grace as an unmerited gift.

Many people have a problem with the idea of murderers and rapists coming to Christ in prison and obtaining salvation just because they have accepted this grace. This is sometimes hard for us to swallow because we tend to impose our system of justice upon God. This may be hard for you, but God wants the soul of a murderer as much as He wants yours. Grace is for everyone who is earnestly willing to accept Christ as their Savior, regardless of the sins they have committed in the past. This seems unbelievable, but in referring to this Christ said that with God everything is possible.

I say this because you may consider yourself unworthy of this grace and love. We are all sinners and God holds you on the same level of the saints if you accept the grace He is offering you. When you first experience God's Spirit within you and realize that you have been given this awesome gift of grace, you do feel unworthy! But remember the definition of grace – you are not worthy, but God loves you and wants you in His eternal loving presence anyway.

So, the question then becomes if we are saved by grace and not by our works, once we accept this grace does that mean we can sin all we want and still be saved? Well let's talk about that. If you accept this grace (justifying grace) and fully realize the significance of Christ's sacrifice for you, then you'll want to spend your life doing your best to live according to God's will. This is called sanctifying grace. It is living your life in gratitude for this gift of grace from God.

If you accept God's gift of grace and don't move on toward sanctifying grace, then this is "cheap grace". It cheapens God's grace if you don't live your life according to God's will after you have been given this grace. It is the charge of every Christian to spend the rest of their lives turning this cheap grace into expensive grace by striving toward a life of perfection in Christ.

What about the millions of people in the world who will never have the opportunity of hearing about Christ? Will they have salvation? This has been debated throughout the ages and I can only offer my opinion. I believe that everyone in the world who is saved, whether they realize it or not, is saved because of God's grace through Jesus Christ. I believe that God judges us based on our exposure to this grace. In other words, if we were never given the opportunity to accept or reject the grace offered through Christ, I don't believe that God holds that against us. However, if we are given that opportunity, then I believe He does allow us to reject Him and bear the consequences of our rejection.

I personally don't believe that hell is a place where

you are tortured and burned for eternity. I do believe that hell is an existence where there is no God. This in and of itself would be eternal anguish in my opinion, but it is the result of our rejection of God.

I said that we tend to impose our worldly concept of justice upon God in terms of how we think people should be judged. In God's eyes, the worst thing someone can do is to declare that they do not need Him and to reject the sacrifice made by His Son, Jesus Christ. I don't mean to sound overbearing or fanatical here, but it really boils down to this. Remember, God never rejects us. We reject Him and because He loves us so much He gives us free will to do that. We just have to live with the consequences of this decision if we reject God.

Probably the most famous hymn of all time is "Amazing Grace". Most people know the first verse: "Amazing Grace, how sweet the sound, that saved a wretch like me. I once was lost, but now I'm found. T'was blind, but now I see." The writer of this hymn obviously rejoiced upon discovering that his sins were forgiven by the grace of God.

Realizing that you have salvation by the grace of God is so empowering. It also lifts the fear of death off of your shoulders. Knowing that you will triumph over death, just as Christ did, by accepting Christ is a peace of mind unequalled by anything else.

Many people fear death. They fear the unknown. They want to know exactly what will happen when they die. This is perfectly natural because we naturally fear the unknown. No one remembers the moments in their mother's womb before they were born, but suppose for a moment you did have a cognitive awareness. You are warm and comfortable in your mother's womb and totally relaxed by the sound of your mother's beating heart. This is the only world you have ever known.

All of a sudden contractions begin and the walls all around you are shaking and you are being forced out into a cold, unknown environment with bright lights, loud sounds and people with masks hovering over you. The moment we are being born has to be terrifying to us. We naturally resist. But we have to "die" to the world of our mother's womb in order to be born into this world, which is much more vast and wonderful than we could have ever known in the womb. Still, we were terrified to die to the only existence that we had ever known and we resisted change.

That is exactly how it is going into the next world.

We have to die from this world in order to be born into God's promised kingdom, which will be much more vast and wonderful than we could ever imagine while we're living here. We don't know exactly what will happen the moment we die and we don't know the details of the next world but Jesus said, "You will be with me", and knowing this is all that matters. You know that if you are where He is, this is where you want to be. God brought you into this world without you having anything to do with it. Trust Him to bring you into the next world, which is His ultimate plan.

In summary, we are saved by God's grace through accepting Jesus Christ, not by our good works. What we do is important, but our motivation should be a response to what God has done for us, not trying to earn salvation from God by doing good works. Paul says that it is very important to follow the Ten Commandments and other aspects of God's law, but following the law is what we should want to do as gratitude for God's gift of grace. Following God's law is not our means of salvation. That implies that we do it ourselves and undermines the significance of Christ dying on the cross for us.

We are given the free will to either accept or reject this gift of grace that God has given us. The way we accept this gift is to acknowledge and believe in the sacrifice of Christ and realize that He took the punishment for our sins by being crucified. The other part of accepting this grace is to believe that Christ was resurrected and therefore triumphed over death so that we could triumph over death as well. Accept this, and you are justifying grace. Live a life of gratitude for this gift of grace and you are sanctifying grace. That's all you have to do and that's what it's all about!

Chapter Six

Prayer

*T*here are many people who simply don't know how to pray. There are also many people who don't know or understand the purpose of prayer and therefore have no idea of the power of prayer.

What is prayer? Prayer is our oral communication with God. It is simply talking to God. Any relationship is based on communication and the more you pray the closer your relationship is with God.

So how do you pray? Many people have heard

formal prayers in public and feel very uncomfortable praying to God because they don't feel they know how. They can't ramble off the canned phrases that seem to be used so eloquently by the professionals in invocations at public events. Where do you start and what does God want to hear?

You should pray to God in a conversational tone, just like you were talking to your best friend. God wants you to speak to Him from your heart. He does not hold you to any high expectations. He just wants to hear from you. Your prayers shouldn't be said as if they were canned. They should be informal and sincere. Remember that God knows what you need more than you do.

Although there are no set rules for praying, there are a few things you should consider. Jesus gave us His outline for an appropriate format of praying to God in the form of The Lord's Prayer, which is as follows:

"Our Father, who art in heaven, hallowed be Thy name. Thy kingdom come, Thy will be done, on earth as it is in heaven. Give us this day, our daily bread, and forgive us our trespasses, as we forgive those who trespass against us. And lead us not into temptation, but deliver us from evil. For Thine is the

kingdom, the power and the glory forever. Amen."
Let's analyze a few lines in this powerful prayer.
Obviously, when you are praying you don't have to
use the same format every time and certainly don't
have to use the King James language. Your prayers
should be in conversational language. Nevertheless,
let's look at Jesus' example. The first 2 sentences are
very interesting. Note that Jesus acknowledges God
in heaven and then begins the prayer by praising
God. He does not begin by immediately asking for
something, but by praising God.

I think many people overlook this very important
aspect of prayer. One of the primary purposes of
praying should be to give thanks and praise to the
Lord. Then, move on to your concerns. When Jesus
says, "Thy will be done", that is probably the high-
est level you can attain in your praying. Basically,
you are pouring our your heart to God in prayer for
your needs and concerns but the bottom line is that
you are telling God that you pray for His will to be
done, even if it goes against what you think is best
for you. This is a very hard level to achieve and
requires great trust in God.

Also note that Jesus says to ask for forgiveness and
to acknowledge that you forgive others who have
harmed you. We'll talk about forgiveness later,

which is one of the most important and difficult principles of Christianity. He also says, "Give us this day,
our daily bread." I think we can all learn from this.
Basically Jesus is saying that we should live for
today. He doesn't complain about the lack of bread
we had in the past or ask for big storage bins of grain
for tomorrow's bread. He is asking for God to provide our needs for today.

When you begin to pray, start by praising God and
then just simply talk to God. Thank God, share your
concerns with God, and it's OK to ask God for things
if your motivation is pure. I want to address a couple
of issues on this subject of praying for things or for
things to happen or not happen.

Does prayer really change things? Why does God
respond to some prayers and not others? Is it OK to
share your petty concerns with God in prayer when
there are children in the hospital dying of cancer? In
other words, when there are those out in the world
with real problems, how can we bother God with our
concerns that seem insignificant to what some people are facing?

First of all, I'm absolutely convinced that in many
instances prayer does change things. I think prayer is
one of the most powerful forces in our universe. I

believe that when we get to heaven, our joy will be initially squelched a bit because one of the things that will be revealed to us is what could have happened if we had prayed more.

God longs for a relationship with us and that relationship is developed through prayer to Him. Can a simple prayer to God actually motivate God to physically intervene in this world and change things? I think the answer to that is absolutely yes. The examples are all through the Bible and I truly feel that we can sometimes move God so greatly with our sincere prayers to Him that He in fact decides to intervene in a situation.

But, beyond physically intervening such as healing through prayer, praying will always help with your internal struggles. If you pray for patience, courage and inner strength, or for God's forgiveness, these types of prayers work every time. God will always strengthen your inner spirit and many times your problems are solved this way.

So why does God respond to some prayers and not others? We've all known situations in our lives where those who were prayed for were healed and others who were prayed for were not. I have no answer for you to this very difficult question. I can only offer this. We cannot see the whole picture from our perspective. Certainly God always wants us to pray and certainly God is always there with us during our suffering. Many times He chooses not to physically intervene with our prayers for healing and it's hard to understand why. We simply have to have faith in God and to trust our God, knowing that even if we are not healed that He is there with us and has a plan for us beyond our knowledge.

Sometimes my young children will ask something of me and my answer is "no". Their young minds cannot understand my reasoning and they cannot understand, from their perspective, how a loving parent can deny a request that they feel is certainly in their best interest. At this point a parent can only say to them that some day they will understand why one's decision was for their own good. It is impossible for a child to understand and know everything that is for her own good. Children tend to think very short term and don't see the bigger picture that you do.

I think one blessing in children is being shown how His relationship with us is so similar. It gives you an idea of how much love a parent (God) can have for His children (us). This also demonstrates that as God's children, we cannot know the greater picture of what is for our own good. Many times when we pray for something and God has to say "no", I believe He is lovingly saying to us that some day we'll understand His decision as to why it was His will.

There are many who believe that God will always heal them if their faith is strong enough. I take exception to this way of thinking. This is using "faith" to manipulate God's actions and this whole way of thinking is fundamentally wrong. Yes, it is OK to pray for healing and many times the power of prayer will heal you. But it is even more important to pray for inner strength and perseverance and for God to help you through your struggle. This prayer will always be answered. And also remember Jesus' words, "Thy will be done".

Some feel it is fine to pray to God for blessings of material possessions. There is a common belief, even among some of the Christian community, that if we go to church, live our lives in a Christian manner and pray like we should that God will bless us with money, health, a big house and two sports cars in the garage. This thinking is also flawed. God never gives us material blessings just for the sake of materialism. If He blesses us in this manner, He expects us to use these blessings to be a blessing to others.

We are always blessed to be a blessing, not to simply

enjoy our material possessions ourselves. We are to acknowledge to God in prayer that everything we have comes from Him and to give Him genuine gratitude for the many blessings that He showers upon us daily. We are also expected to give away a portion of which has been given to us.

Yes, it is OK to come to God with your petty concerns. God wants to hear from you no matter what. If you have genuine small concerns that you want to take to God in prayer for guidance, I believe that is certainly fine with Him. Just be careful about your motivations and remember that you are not talking to a genie. God is not there to grant your every wish. Remember that God knows what you really need far more than you do.

Your prayer skills will get better with practice. Your prayers will flow better and you'll feel more and more comfortable talking to God. By praying, you'll feel closer to God because the greatest benefit of prayer is God's Holy Spirit within you. Pray creatively, emotionally and genuinely. And after you pray, the next step is to listen.

Learning how to listen to God is also a skill that comes from thoughtful prayer. God reveals Himself to you in many ways. When you seek God's help for

guidance through prayer, you will get the "gut" feeling that will send you in the proper direction of
God's will.

I do believe that the stronger your faith is, the better
your prayer results will be for the inner healings that
you are requesting from God. You will always have
more inner peace, strength, courage, wisdom and
perseverance if you have stronger faith because these
are the most powerful results of faithful prayer.

I also believe that praying for others carries a lot of
weight with God. God looks for your true motivation
and certainly hears prayers that are unselfish. Pray
for the well-being of your family and friends. Pray
for your country and for all of the people hurting in
the world right now. Pray for others to find God. You
may never know it, but you may change someone's
life for the better just by your prayer.

If you haven't ever prayed much, how do you start?
I would suggest that you simply open your heart to
God and tell Him what is on your mind. Tell Him
that you want to get to know Him better and to help
show you how. Although at times it may seem like a
one-sided conversation and a one-way relationship,
God will answer you if you earnestly listen. It may
not be an immediate answer. He may want you to get

into the habit of praying daily for a while before He answers you. But God will reveal Himself to you if you seek Him, and when He does you will feel it and know it as strongly as anything you have ever felt.

There is no question that the more you pray, the better you get at it. Also, the more you pray in front of others, the better you get at that too. Praying in front of others, such as saying grace at the family reunion, can be very intimidating. But God wants you to push yourself, because that's how you grow. Sometimes you have to make yourself pray in front of others when the situation is appropriate and little by little it gets easier. The Bible says that there is great power whenever two or three people come to God in prayer together. I think this is true because a prayer of this nature requires a special level that doesn't even exist in private prayer to God or in a large group.

The Bible says that we should pray without ceasing. Does that mean pray all of the time? In a sense, yes it does. You strive to eventually get to the point where you are always in communion with God and walking in His spirit. Your whole existence permeates with the Spirit within you that is the result of a constant awareness of God's presence in your life. You begin to see God working in every aspect of your life. You begin to recognize what He has been trying to tell you all along. In this sense, your life becomes one big "prayer", which is a closeness to God 24 hours a day, 7 days a week.

Chapter 7

The Holy Spirit

I've already said that Christians believe in a tri-une God; that is, God the Father, God the Son, and God the Holy Spirit...one God, three persons. Up until now, we have talked quite a bit about the first two elements of the Trinity, but not much about the Holy Spirit. The concept of the Holy Spirit (sometimes referred to as the "Holy Ghost" in Southern churches or as "The Advocate" or "The Counselor" by Jesus in the Bible) is a bit difficult to explain.

By definition, the Holy Spirit is God's presence all around us and within us on this earth. When God guides us and manifests Himself in us, it is done by His Holy Spirit. It is God's Holy Spirit that changes our lives. It is God's Holy Spirit that moves us to seek Him out and to do His will.

When God acts directly in our world, it is His Spirit, His Being, that is doing this. The Old Testament refers to "the Spirit of God" many times, particularly when referring to God actively engaging a human being to do His will. In the Old Testament, the Holy Spirit is usually referred to when God puts His Spirit on someone for a specific purpose.

In the New Testament, the role of the Holy Spirit changes greatly. When Jesus was predicting His imminent death to His disciples, obviously they didn't want to hear such talk. But Jesus was very clear when He said that His work on this earth was almost finished. He told them that He must die in order to fulfill His purpose but that His Father would soon send "The Advocate" to always be with them after His death on this earth. In other words, Jesus was telling His disciples that after His physical death, God would send to them His Holy Spirit, which would always be with them while they are on this earth.

This Spirit is God's Spirit within us and is God's gift while we are here, which is obtained through Jesus Christ. That is how the Trinity is all tied together. The gift of eternal salvation and God's Holy Spirit while we are on this earth is available to us by accepting Christ. No longer does God pick and choose who He will give His Spirit to for a specific purpose, as in the Old Testament. Now His Spirit belongs to everyone through Christ.

When God begins working in your life, this is His Spirit working within you. Part of being a Christian is learning how to "let go and let God." You may have met some Christians who have alluded to God leading them in certain directions in their lives and you're thinking they sound like a kook. I have to tell you, however, when God is working in your life, you know it. Sometimes we are able to get through extremely difficult times that seem overwhelming, sometimes we're able to rise to the occasion and go beyond our normal ability to reach someone else and sometimes we experience a situation that we call "Divine intervention". In all of these situations, we realize that there was a power greater than us at work in our lives. This is an example of experiencing God's Holy Spirit.

Our relationship with God is actually developed

through our relationship with Christ and with the Holy Spirit. When we feel closer to God through prayer and experience, we are experiencing God through His Spirit. It is God's Spirit within us that helps us better understand scripture and better understand God as we grow in our spiritual journey. It is God's Spirit that enables me to write these words and enables us to speak to others about Christ.

Christ told His disciples not to worry about what they would say if they were captured and had to answer pointed questions about their affiliation with Him. He also told them not to worry about how they would explain their experience with Jesus to others. Jesus told them that the Holy Spirit would take over and help them with the words. Whenever you are doing God's work, His Spirit is there with you giving you the strength, courage, knowledge and wisdom that you need.

Although Jesus Christ and the Holy Spirit are the two facets of God that come into play in His relationship with humankind, you must understand that both Jesus and the Holy Spirit have always existed and will always exist. God has always existed in three forms, eternally backwards and eternally forwards.

It is very difficult to comprehend how God can have

no beginning or end because our minds are constructed to only be able to conceive of a beginning and an end. In our human terms, we look at time as linear. However, God transcends time and He is in fact the Creator of time and is in control of time. Christians believe that God the Father, God the Son and God the Holy Spirit have always existed as God and will always exist as God. This is a difficult concept to understand and grasp at first and a thorough discussion of this subject is beyond the scope of this book. The more you read the Bible and other Christian literature, the more you will understand God in three forms.

The concept of the Trinity is something Christians believe but cannot fully explain because part of their belief is through experience rather than simple knowledge. Christians are certainly not claiming that there are three separate Gods. There is definitely only one God, but this God exists in three forms. A triune God makes for a much more personal, loving God to humankind.

Most people have a conscience, to varying degrees. We refer to our conscience as that inner voice that tells us right from wrong. It is our conscience that gives us guilt when we do something we know is wrong. Is our conscience really the Holy Spirit of

God? Christians think not. Our conscience is shaped by our life experiences. If we seek out God, His Holy Spirit will help shape our conscience. Our conscience and the Holy Spirit are not one in the same. However, as we allow God's Holy Spirit within us, our conscience conforms to His will for our lives. Our core beliefs become more in alignment with God through the workings of the Holy Spirit in our lives.

In the New Testament Paul writes a lot about the "fruits of the Spirit". When the Holy Spirit is in our lives, we bear good fruit. He mentions that the fruit of the Spirit is love, joy, peace, patience, kindness, generosity, faithfulness, gentleness, and self-control. The Holy Spirit enables us to live like Christians should, as examples to others, which makes the world a better place.

Paul also speaks of spiritual gifts. Spiritual gifts are gifts from the Holy Spirit to us, which should be used to strengthen the faith of others. Paul says that all Christians make up the "body of Christ". Are the eyes more important than the ears or the mouth? All parts of the body are necessary and we all have these gifts, which can be used to strengthen the Christian church and the body of Christ. Some people have the gift of teaching about God, others have the gift of administrative leadership, some the gift of music and still others have the gift of dutifully volunteering for whatever is needed.

Gifts of the Spirit are used to bring others to God and to strengthen their faith. People who use their spiritual gifts are doing their part to build the faith community and to serve as faithful examples to others. God has always used people to reach other people. If you look at the predominant people in the Bible, you'll see that He uses ordinary people to deliver an extraordinary message. Most of the icons in the Bible certainly didn't regard themselves as such at the time. If you think that you have nothing to offer others and do not have any spiritual gifts, you are dead wrong. You have gifts that you don't even know about, and as your faith grows so does God's living Spirit within you and your special gifts to bring others to Christ will emerge.

Realizing and developing your spiritual gifts is just one way that the Holy Spirit will empower you. God acting in your life will give you a zest for life that you never had before. The Holy Spirit will spur you into action. If you are willing to accept what God has to offer you through Christ, then He will give you His Spirit. His Spirit will work in your life in accordance with His will, if you just pray, listen and obey. So, why do we separate God from the Spirit of

God? Why do we look at God's presence within us and all around us as a separate facet of God? Jesus is very clear when He tells the disciples that God's Holy Spirit will be given to them after Jesus leaves this earth. He refers to the Spirit as part of God, but as an element of God's being that is separate than God the Father. The Holy Spirit therefore has a very distinct role as part of the living God. Christians revere God the Father as Creator, God the Son as Redeemer and God the Holy Spirit as Sustainer. And it is through God the Son, Jesus Christ, that we are able to come into the presence of God the Father and God the Holy Spirit.

So when you pray, are you praying to the Father, Son, or Holy Spirit? Most of us think in terms of God the Father when we are praying, but actually you are praying to all three. God is an all-powerful, multi-faceted and complex Being and we relate to His three "persons" in different ways. In our human terms, we have a personal relationship with Jesus Christ. We can identify with Christ as a human being and Christ takes us by the hand and introduces us to the other two elements of God.

For some, it is easier to understand how the Holy Spirit of God can be looked at as a separate facet of God but it is more difficult to see God's Son as part of God Himself. When Jesus prayed to God, was He praying to Himself? Actually, Jesus the man was praying as a human being, as the human Son of God. Jesus the God was and is God in human form. Jesus said that the Father was in Him and He was in the Father. For earthly purposes, He is the Son of God but for Divine purposes He is the part of God that reaches out to us as a human being and makes us right with God through His grace.

People come to Christ in many different ways. For some, it is a life-changing event that takes place and immediately they are changed forever. Many people can pinpoint exactly the moment they decided to give their life to Christ. For others, it is a much more gradual process. In either case, those who do will eventually experience an inner feeling which may come and go but is very powerful and difficult to explain. You feel a certain "high" and you know it comes from God. It may be a feeling or a message you are hearing that everything is going to be OK. It may be a new awareness that you are being guided in a way that you weren't before. Sometimes people experience this and are over-whelmed or even overconfident. When this happens to you, just remember that you are just experiencing God's Holy Spirit that people have been experiencing and writing about for 2,000 years!

Chapter 8

Suffering is Real,
Even for Christians

※

*I*t has been suggested that if any one person could see all of the suffering going on in the world at any given point in time, it would cause insanity in that person. The human brain is not equipped to see and feel firsthand the sum total of all of the suffering in the world. When we hear about terrible things happening, our defense mechanisms kick in and we simply shut our emotions down. We hear about these things and have long since developed our internal response of just chalking it up as another unfortunate statistic in a big, cruel world.

But God, being all-powerful and all-knowing, does see, feel and experience the sum total of all of the suffering in the world every moment of every day. When you think about this you really wonder how a God who loves people can allow such misery and evil to exist. We feel God is in control of these things and we therefore blame God for the suffering in a world which He created.

We may acknowledge that a good amount of the suffering in the world is of our own doing. God doesn't create drug addicts or cause wars. Man's inhumanity to man has long been studied and one can hardly blame God for suffering as a result of the free will acts of human beings.

But what about when a child dies of cancer? Or what about all of the starving people in the world? What about earthquakes, floods and other natural disasters that kill thousands? What about birth defects and unexplained accidents? Why doesn't God stop this and even if much of the evil in our world is man-made, why does God allow such evil to exist? Why is life so hard?

This chapter will attempt to address some of these questions from a Christian perspective. Again, I have to admit to you that if given the chance there are many questions I would like to ask God. I certainly don't have all of the answers. I have a pretty big file called the "mystery of God" file, which things go that I can't explain or understand.

However, I have been blessed with being able to develop a Christian perspective of life. When you're truly able to look at life through the lens of Christ, then life takes on a different meaning and many questions are answered. Some of the answers aren't what you want to hear. Nevertheless, it is important that you come to grips with some of these difficult questions if you are going to get anywhere in your search for spiritual truth.

Let me start with a bold statement. I may not have all of the answers to the difficult questions pertaining to the suffering and injustices of this world, but I am sure of one thing. This life on this earth is not what it's all about. This life is certainly not the "be all to end all". For lack of a better term, this life is "boot camp" for what is to come when we leave this world for God's eternal kingdom.

Your first step in coming to grips with your struggles

of human suffering in the world is to realize that our suffering on this earth is a blink of an eye in the grand scheme of things. Nowhere in the Bible does God ever promise us heaven on earth. For some reason, we are meant to be put through this boot camp first.

Yes, there can be some positive results from our suffering. When we suffer, it often builds our character and heightens our compassion for the plight of our fellow, human being. However, sometimes there is no positive aspect. It's just plain terrible and there is no good that can come out of it. Not in this imperfect world.

We can be basically happy individuals, if we're lucky. If you have Christ in your life, you can actually be joyful (which is better and even longer-lasting than happiness). But if you live long enough you'll realize that perpetual bliss in this life is simply impossible. There are too many hardships and struggles and there is too much pain in this world for anyone to have the capability of being in utopia all of the time. Actually, remember that while we are on this earth, we are separated from God. We can strive for a good and fulfilling life, to be sure. Don't get me wrong, true joy and happiness can come from a personal relationship with Christ. But as long as we are here in this world and not where God is, we'll never be able to have it all.

If I've totally depressed you by now, please don't abandon me yet. This chapter is actually going to turn into a very uplifting message, I hope. The first message I want to stress is that God loves you, no matter what. No matter what happens to you, God loves you. There is nothing you could have ever done in the past that could make God love you any less and there is nothing you can ever do to make God love you any more. His very presence makes our suffering OK and gives it a purpose, in the long run.

This is best illustrated in the book of Job, in the Old Testament. The book of Job tells a story that at first may seem very disturbing to you, but upon further examination is comforting. Briefly, I'll tell you the story. Job was a very righteous man and was very blessed by the Lord. He had a large loving family and many material possessions for his time. The story goes that one day Satan came to God and proclaimed that there were no righteous people left on God's earth. When God pointed out Job to Satan, Satan retorted that Job was righteous as long as he had all of God's blessings. But Satan said in essence, "God, if you allow me to take away everything he has and loves and let me cause him great physical suffering, he'll curse your name."

The first disturbing element of this story is that God takes Satan up on his offer and, to summarize, all of Job's possessions are destroyed, his family is all killed and Satan causes painful boils to cover Job's entire body. You can imagine the grief Job was feeling. The common Hebrew thought of that time was that if bad things happened to you, it was because you had angered God. Very much of this eloquent book of Job consists of his friends trying to comfort and reason with him. They were saying that he had to have done something to anger God and Job kept insisting that he was innocent and that God simply had the wrong suspect.

Job never cursed God, but he did cry out to God for a one on one confrontation. Job was granted an opportunity that few in the history of the world have been afforded. He got his wish for a face to face with The Almighty. Job pled his case to God, saying that he had always been faithful and obedient and that God must have the wrong guy. Why would God punish him like this? Why would God cause him so much hurt, pain and sorrow? If he had to be tortured like this, why was he even born?

God hears Job without interrupting and then it's God's turn to reply. Here's where it gets interesting. Instead of explaining to Job the reasoning behind what happened and to tell Job that he had passed the test, God actually has a very terse reply. God basically says, "So, you think you know everything about the way the world should be, huh? Where were you when I made the earth and the stars and the heavens and where were you when I made the plants and the birds and every living thing on the planet?" Then the message that God conveys to Job in a very powerful way is "I AM GOD."

Job drops to his knees and cries to God, "Who am I to question you, Lord?" And then Job experiences a comfort He has never experienced before. Even after Job had gone through all of that suffering, he didn't need an explanation from God after all. The very awesome presence of God was enough for Job. He was left with an overwhelming feeling of "Wow! That was God!"

The story ends with God blessing Job with a new loving family and children and with more wealth than he ever had before and he ended up living a long and happy life. But this happy ending is really only a minute point of the story. The important points are (1) God doesn't cause our suffering, but He does allow it to happen for a reason that we cannot know or understand, (2) God is all-powerful and in control, (3) God is all-loving and just in the end.

The Bible is full of people who knew hard times. Many of the icons of the New Testament were executed just for their Christian faith (ie., Paul and Peter). There is no question that Jesus identified with the lame, the sick and the despised. Jesus embodied compassion for the suffering of others. There is no way that you can look at Christ as a part of God and not see that God has compassion for our suffering. Please believe that God suffers right along with us, as Christ suffered for us.

There are those who say that since God made the world and since evil exists in the world, that God in effect created the evil. Actually the evil in the world is the result of the absence of people truly knowing and obeying God. We tend to always think of the universe in opposites such as hot and cold and light and darkness. But, scientifically, cold is not the opposite of heat; it is merely the absence of heat. You can't measure cold, only heat. The same is true for light and darkness. Darkness does not exist other than as the absence of light. I tend to look at good and evil and morality and immorality the same way. Evil and immorality are not opposites of good and morality; they are simply the results of the absence of good or morality, which is a result of the absence of God.

When the world chooses to be without God, the result is the absence of God, which leads to a world full of evil and suffering.

There is some good that can come out suffering. I mentioned earlier that it heightens our compassion and awareness of the plight of others. As I write this book, three years ago my 34 year-old wife was diagnosed with breast cancer. She went through surgeries and follow up visits and, by the grace of God, she has been free of cancer since then. But since that difficult time, you better believe that our awareness of breast cancer everywhere around us has greatly intensified. People came out of the woodwork to comfort us and tell us their breast cancer story. The love and support of our family and friends was overwhelming. Since then Paula has counseled others and volunteered at her oncologist's office. Her inner strength and character is much stronger and she is the type person that people come to for moral support during their difficult times. Yes, if she had the choice she would surely choose not to have had breast cancer. But, some good did come from this traumatic event.

Our pain can bring us closer to God. When life just rolls along with no speed bumps, quite often we put God on the back burner. But let sorrow and pain

into our lives, and we come running to Him. God
wants us to run to Him during our difficult times.
Christians are often called to suffer, as Christ suffered, so that we'll have the strengthened character
to help ease the suffering of others in the world.
There is a line in an old hymn which is so instruc-
tive. "Let sorrow do its work, come grief and pain;
sweet are Thy messengers, sweet their refrain;
when they can sing with me, more love, O Christ to
Thee; more love to Thee; more love to Thee."[1]

Next to spreading the Word of God, there is no
stronger calling to Christians than mission work.
Christian organizations throughout the world exist to
reach out, bring people in, build people up and send
people out. Christians view the suffering of the world
as an opportunity to come to Christ and as a respon-
sibility to ease suffering by serving others.

The book of Revelation in the New Testament is very
difficult to read and understand but it has a powerful
message to Christians who are suffering. During that
time, not only did Christians face disease, war,
famine, etc., they also suffered tremendous persecution just for their religious beliefs. The writer of
Revelation continually reminds us that we will suffer
in this imperfect world, but to hang tough and keep
our faith strong, because in the end we will be in

God's kingdom for eternity.

Most of the suffering in the world is a direct result of human beings. The next time you look at the world and wonder how God can allow such hardships to go on, ask yourself, "How can WE allow these things to go on?" Mankind is stronger and better and more humane because of the famine and disease we have been forced to fight since the dawn of our existence. Although we have come a long way, there is still so much more we can do. The next chapter on Christian service will address how one person can make a difference.

As beautiful as this world is, if this were all there really was then how depressing would that be? If you only look at the "here and now" as your grand scheme of things, then you will never have peace of mind. This world just does not offer peace of mind without understanding the end of the story. Christ came to earth to suffer as an example as well as die for us so that we may have more to our story than just this life on earth. When you truly understand this, it does help ease your pain and sorrow and give you peace.

What about loneliness? This is perhaps one of the hardest aspects of life. You lose a spouse, you get a divorce, the children move out of the house, or you lose touch with family and friends. Everyone is lonely, to a certain extent. We come into this world alone and we leave it alone and we are all individuals who have to live our individual lives. Someone once said, "We're all in this together, all by ourselves." Christ wants you to know that He is your best friend. A personal relationship with Jesus Christ will mean that you are never really alone. Knowing this will not end your loneliness, but it certainly will help.

Do you want to know the best cure for loneliness after you have made Christ your best friend? Get outside of yourself. Rather than sit around the house feeling sorry for yourself, get out and get involved by serving others in some way. You'll find that there are others in the world who are lonely just like you, and by reaching out to them you will cure your loneliness as well as theirs!

When life gets hard, you can't bear it alone. You are not meant to bear it alone. Go to God in prayer and admit to Him that you cannot handle your situation and you're turning everything over to Him. Ask Christ to come into your life and help you cope. Then, believe that He will help you and I promise He will. Christianity is not a crutch or a sign of weakness for those who can't handle life's trials and tribulations on their own. Christianity is the source of strength that we need to make it through this boot camp we call life.

---

[1] *More Love to Thee* by Elizabeth P. Prentiss, 1869.

Chapter 9

Christian Service, Humility and Forgiveness— All One Package

*J*esus Christ came to serve, not be served. The Jewish people were not expecting a humble servant as their messiah. Jesus washed the feet of His disciples, which was the job of a servant, to demonstrate how we should be. As Christians, we are called upon to follow the example of Christ. So, if you're trying to figure out what it truly means to be a Christian after accepting the Christian beliefs, this chapter will help because it's all about service, humility and forgiveness.

I mentioned earlier in the book that it's not always easy to follow the example of Christ. Quite often the world pushes us in the exact opposite direction. We are trained to be selfish, fiercely competitive and self-preserving. We are programmed to be survivalist in a "dog eat dog" world. Being "worldly" is considered a virtue in our culture and we are absolutely out of control with our materialism in this country.

Somehow our modern competitive culture has grown to believe that one must step on others to get ahead in life. The "nice guys finish last" adage seems to be the common belief. Some people actually look at business and life as a zero sum game. In other words, for someone to win, someone else has to lose.

But Zig Ziglar had it right when he said, "You can have everything you want by helping the other person get everything he or she wants." Nothing will make you more successful and happy in the true sense of the definition than living this philosophy. And living this philosophy is in accordance with the example Christ set for us.

We humans are vain creatures and we have big egos. We want recognition for our good works. We're easily put on the defensive when someone criticizes us and we are aggressive and hot-tempered when someone angers us. We are prejudiced towards those who are different than we and we have little desire to try to understand them. All of these characteristics are part of our human condition and the reason we are all sinners. They are also everything Jesus is not.

When you become a Christian, you will experience a shift in the way you view the world. It all begins with what is in your heart. Although you'll continue to fail and be imperfect, your heart will still desire to be more Christ-like. Having your heart in the right place means that your motivations are pure. In His teachings, Jesus is very concerned with what is in your heart because this is where it all begins.

When you realize that you are nothing but a lowly sinner without Christ, you will have this change of heart and this will break down the barriers to let God into your life completely. When this happens, you'll be ready to serve God by serving others. You'll be a more humble and authentic person. You'll start to focus on what is truly important in life, such as how much love you can give to others every day.

Let's talk about materialism for just a moment, because I'm just as guilty as anyone in this regard. Our society wants to keep up with the Jones', and we want everything now. That is why most Americans don't save money and so many Americans are swimming in credit card debt. Jesus said a couple of very interesting things pertaining to money and possessions. He said that in the kingdom of God the last would be first and the first would be last. What do you suppose He meant by that? He also said that it would be easier for a camel to jump through the eye of a needle than for a rich person to get into heaven. Now that's disturbing! What do you think that statement really means?

I think Christ was first trying to say that we should be extremely careful about what we treasure and value. One of the most important of the Ten Commandments is "You shall have no other gods before me", and this means that money and wealth should not be your ultimate goal in life. You should first seek God and He should be your first priority. Jesus was merely pointing out that those with an abundance of material possessions quite often prioritize these possessions over God and their greed leads to misplaced priorities.

Jesus said that where your heart is, your treasure will

be also. Is your treasure money and possessions or is your treasure a loving relationship with God? In your search to develop your spiritual self, you need to examine your priorities in life. What do you think about? How do you spend your time? How do you spend your money? Answering these questions honestly will help in your self-assessment of where your treasure truly lies.

Is Jesus saying that money is evil and it's bad to be rich? Actually, I don't believe He is necessarily saying that. If used appropriately money can be a real blessing to others. You can be a righteous rich person and still have your priorities in the right place. From my observation, it is just harder for people of great wealth to continue to realize where their blessings come from and to keep their priorities in order and their greed in check. The Bible says that you cannot serve both God and money. Money is simply a means to an end and should be viewed as your blessing from God, which should be used to better the world.

Tithing is a Biblical principal that teaches us to give a portion of the money we have been blessed with to God. This means giving 10% of your gross income to church and charity. Giving at a "gross" level is an individual thing to compute. For example, a farmer is somewhat different than a salaried person. Christians consider their wealth and possessions as coming from and belonging to God. You cannot talk about the Christian life without stressing the importance of giving because tithing is so important.

In our Christian service to others, we are supposed to give out of our poverty. If we have a lot of money but very little time, our poverty is time so we're supposed to give time in addition to money. You're supposed to give until it hurts by giving out of your poverty and you're not supposed to tell anyone about your giving. Anonymous donors are true givers. You should harbor your giving in your heart and not worry about recognition from others. Again, watch your motivation and examine your heart. This is hard to do, because it goes against human nature. But you should give out of your love for God and God's people and not for recognition.

One of the more powerful teaching illustrations of Jesus is His reference to dividing the goats and sheep. He said that some people would be considered like goats and would not be judged favorably because when He was hungry they didn't feed Him and when He was thirsty they didn't give him anything to drink. When He was cold they didn't clothe him. When His stunned hearers asked Jesus about not attending to His needs, Jesus said that upon seeing that needy person on the street and ignoring him, they were ignoring Jesus.

Then our Lord turned to those He called sheep and said they were blessed because when He was hungry they fed Him and when He was thirsty they gave Him drink and when He was cold they clothed Him. When these people tell Jesus that they didn't remember doing this for Him, He reminded them of when they did help those in need. He said that when you help them, you're helping Him.

One of the more distinguishing characteristics of Christianity, as opposed to the other religions of the world, is how Christians view service and humility. The Christian philosophy is not "an eye for an eye" but rather it's "turn the other cheek". Also, the goal of being a great Christian is not what level of spirituality you can attain for yourself. The goal of being a great Christian is how much you can humble yourself before the Lord and serve Him by serving others. Quite often, this is a harder sale because we don't live in a society that teaches us humility.

But I will tell you this. There is no greater letdown in life than the realization that the accumulation of money and material possessions alone will not make you happy. If you spend years trying to accumulate "stuff" and ignoring your relationships and your spiritual growth, you'll wake up one day realizing how empty your life is and you'll really be able to identify with the writer of Ecclesiastes, King Solomon. Here you had the greatest and most successful king in the history of the Hebrew people. He had taken what his beloved father, King David, had done and turned Israel into an economically booming kingdom for that particular day and time. He had many wives, lots and lots of money, and power. But, his spirit was lacking and he realized that all of these material things were just vanity. He asked, "What is the point of all of this, anyway?" We're here today and gone tomorrow and what we think is so important on this earth really means nothing in the grand scheme of things.

We are put here in this boot camp life to learn how to give, to forgive, to serve, to suffer and to love. We have talked about most of these Christian principles up to this point but haven't said much about forgiveness. Forgiveness is such an important aspect of Christianity that I would be remiss in leaving it out of this work.

We are all forgiven people. We are forgiven of our

sins and we are therefore supposed to forgive others. Remember the Lord's Prayer, "Forgive us our trespasses, as we forgive those who trespass against us". Now, when someone really hurts us, forgiving this person is much easier said than done.

Forgiveness is like grief in that it is a process. When someone hurts you badly, it takes time to forgive and it's very difficult to get yourself to that point. When you do forgive someone, initially it feels like you've lost and they've won. They hurt you and you have forgiven them, so they came out on top. But when you harbor animosity, it is you that gets destroyed on the inside. Hatred and resentment devastates you, not them. And when you forgive, it is you that will ultimately be set free from the bondage of this animosity so you can move on with your life.

When you forgive others, their reaction should be immaterial to your feelings. Whether they thank you for your forgiveness and are genuinely repentant or they mock you and laugh in your face, your feelings should be the same. You have done your part by doing the Christ-like act of forgiving them and what they do with it is their business and of no concern to you. You are now free to move on!

It takes a humble and willing heart to forgive. You

should forgive because you have been forgiven. Ultimately, you will be a better person for it. God will help you forgive. Pray to Him for help in guidance on how to forgive and He will help. Remember that God is the master of forgiving. We sin against Him everyday and He still loves us enough to forgive us but He also expects us to do the same for others.

As a Christian, you are to give and forgive. True Christianity is "dying to self". In other words, being the opposite of selfish. When the world is pulling you another direction, it can be very difficult to maintain this mentality. But as a Christian, you are called to be set apart and to make God the center of your life.

I once heard a notable local minister speaking at our church about his work. He was doing and continues to do wonderful things for the poorest parts of Little Rock. His ministry is to help the needy any way he can. During his speech, he said something very powerful, "If we Christians don't take care of these needs, who will?"

It is our calling to make the world a better place. One person can make such a difference. Just start small. Grow where you are planted. You don't have to solve the world hunger problem or cure cancer. Just find a way you can serve someone else. You'll be amazed at how great you feel and how thankful you'll be when you serve those less able and less fortunate.

Chapter 10

What Now?

I would have to be awfully egotistical to think you
would simply read this book and decide to come
to Christ. As I said in the first chapter, the purpose of
this book is to introduce to you some key concepts of
the Christian faith and hopefully hit a nerve that will
motivate you to seek out more. From here, please
begin reading the Bible, starting with the New
Testament. If nothing else, read it out of sheer interest of what this fascinating book has to say.

You'll need to eventually make some decisions.

First, do you believe that Jesus was and is the only Son of God sent here to redeem us? Do you believe and accept the grace He offers to you? Do you want to go deeper into the Christian faith through prayer, study and church attendance? Do you want to experience God working in your life?

I don't mean to sound overbearing because your faith is a personal thing but you should acknowledge that you will have a decision to make. If you decide to stay where you are, then you've made a decision. If you decide to reject Christianity totally, then you've made a decision to do that. It is my prayer that you continue your search in the direction of Christ.

If you do make the decision to accept the Christian faith, then you have only taken the first step. What it's really all about is living the Christian faith. You'll still sin and make mistakes but you'll continue to strive for perfection with the help of Christ as your friend and example.

As you continue down your spiritual walk, please don't get impatient and try to force it. Don't expect God to speak to you through a burning bush right away. You have to "fall in faith" as you would fall in love. Through prayer, study, church fellowship and listening to God your faith will grow. Remember that

God does promise to reveal Himself to everyone who seeks Him.

You may be curious as to my motivation for writing this book. To be truthful, I can't tell you exactly why other than a burning need to share my faith with others. I truly believe God put it on my heart to share my Christian beliefs with you in hopes of helping you discover your beliefs. If I could turn just one life to Christ, then my efforts would be worth it one hundred times over.

So why believe the Gospel? First, it has to fascinate you that when Jesus left this world, His only followers were a few uneducated very poor people who were terrified that they would be killed for their association with Jesus. He left it up to 11 downtrodden guys to spread the news of His resurrection. Isn't that incredible? It is almost impossible to believe that God hasn't been at work during the evolution of the Christian movement. Christianity has flourished the most during the times when Christians were being persecuted and killed.

There have been some dark spots in the history of Christianity as well. Those who speak poorly of religion tend to bring up the times of the crusades and all of the religious wars throughout the ages. But, I submit to you that the good far outweighs the bad. Human beings need God, and Christ has been the way to God for millions of people the past 2,000 years.

In your search for what to believe, let me implore you not to let church politics tarnish your faith. Don't let people with wacky beliefs scare you away either. There is a reason there are many denominations of the Christian faith. Some views work for some and others serve different models. Personally, I've always preferred the "love them into heaven" rather than "scare them out of hell" approach. The various Christian denominations are really just skin deep. Basically, all Christians believe in the same fundamental truths about Christ. Just choose the church that best suits your needs to serve and worship.

When trying to decide what you believe, examine your heart. Take a close evaluation of what could be getting in the way of your faith growing. Take small steps, but take steps. Don't limit yourself either. If you allow Him, you would be absolutely amazed at what God can do with your life. Don't fear God. Trust Him to lead you down the path that He wants for you. If you seek Him out, you will find Him. This is a truly proven fact!

www.ingramcontent.com/pod-product-compliance
Lightning Source LLC
Chambersburg PA
CBHW020355100426
42812CB00001B/74